CONVERGE
Bible Studies

ENCOUNTERING GRACE

Bible Studies

ENCOUNTERING GRACE

JOSEPH YOO

Abingdon Press

Nashville

ENCOUNTERING GRACE
CONVERGE BIBLE STUDIES

By Joseph Yoo

Library of Congress Cataloging-in-Publication Data has been requested.

ISBN: 978-1-4267-9553-4

Series Editor: Shane Raynor

14 15 16 17 18 19 20 21 22 23—10 9 8 7 6 5 4 3 2 1

Manufactured in the United States of America

CONTENTS

ABOUT THE SERIES

Converge is a series of topical Bible studies based on the Common English Bible translation. Each title in the *Converge* series consists of four studies based around a common topic or theme. *Converge* brings together a unique group of writers from different backgrounds, traditions, and age groups.

HOW TO USE THESE STUDIES

Converge Bible studies can be used by small groups, classes, or individuals. Each study uses a simple format. For the convenience of the reader, the primary Scripture passages are included. In Insight and Ideas, the author of the study explores each Scripture passage, going deeper into the text and helping readers understand how the Scripture connects with the theme of the study. Questions are designed to encourage both personal reflection and group conversation. Some questions may not have simple answers. That's part of what makes studying the Bible so exciting.

Although Bible passages are included with each session, study participants may find it useful to have personal Bibles on hand for referencing other Scriptures. *Converge* studies are designed for use with the Common English Bible; but they work well with any modern, reliable translation.

ONLINE EXTRAS

Converge studies are available in both print and digital formats. Each title in the series has additional components that are available online, including related blog posts and podcasts.

To access the companion materials, visit

http://www.MinistryMatters.com/Converge

Thanks for using *Converge*!

INTRODUCTION

One time when I attended a conference, one of the speakers told us the new thing that his church was going to focus on during the upcoming year: grace.

At first, I couldn't help but be on my high, itinerant horse. *New thing? Focus on? He should be a United Methodist,* I thought. We talk about grace all the time.

It wasn't until I started preparing for this study that I realized that United Methodists—OK, more truthfully, *I—do not* talk about grace all the time. Sure, I preach about grace quite often. But that's different from talking about grace. I've never sat with someone and discussed it or asked thoughtful questions such as, "What should a grace-filled person really look like?" I've never really struggled and wrestled with it. Even worse, at times, I find myself withholding grace more than giving it.

I know about grace—with my head. I learned (memorized, forgot, and re-memorized) Wesley's theology of grace—

prevenient, justifying, and sanctifying grace. And to be honest, most of that was for my ordination papers (and to graduate from seminary). I've read books about grace but mostly for sermon and study preparation.

As I prepared to write this Bible study, I was confronted with how little I've really experienced grace at the heart level. Don't get me wrong, I've encountered grace; but I've always been quick to try to understand it, to make it make sense, instead of just receiving it.

So, here's my confession. This study was an unexpected difficult journey for me. I picked the topic of grace because I thought that it would be easy. There are so many examples of grace in the world and in Scripture; and since "we talk about grace all the time," I figured that I would be OK. I was in for quite an awakening.

Perhaps I've rarely given myself the opportunity to understand grace experientially because I've only wanted to understand it insofar as I needed to in order to teach and preach it. Sometimes knowledge can be used to control. Perhaps my desire to understand grace so that I could explain it better had me trying to control grace. And if I can control grace, it means that I can forgo listening to those pesky words Jesus said: "You received without having to pay. Therefore, give without demanding payment" (Matthew 10:8b).

I have no idea what effect this study will have on you and/or your group, but I pray that meaningful discussions will come from the sessions that lie ahead. We'll begin with one of my favorite stories: Jacob wrestling with God. Then we'll touch on repentance and how grace restores us, followed by how it transforms us and how we sometimes take grace for granted. In the final session, we'll talk about how it's possible for religion to get in the way of grace and how grace often needs to trump our own ideology and theology.

In no way do I claim to be an expert on this topic. I'm woefully underqualified to write this study. But what I am certain of is that grace is a truly amazing and transforming concept. We can't un-see what we've seen through grace. I believe that it leaves a permanent mark on our souls.

My prayer is that this study will serve as a springboard for you to have encounters that will push, nudge, and stretch the beliefs and conceptions you have about grace and faith. May your discussions be filled with God's grace as you grow deeper in faith and in love for God and God's people.

As you set out on this journey, I'm thoroughly grateful that you have allowed me to be a small part of the conversation.

"May you have more and more grace and peace through the knowledge of God and Jesus our Lord" (2 Peter 1:2).

1

WHAT'S IN A NAME?
WHEN GRACE CHANGES EVERYTHING

SCRIPTURE
GENESIS 32:1-32

[1]Jacob went on his way, and God's messengers approached him.
[2]When Jacob saw them, he said, "This is God's camp," and he
named that sacred place Mahanaim.[1] [3]Jacob sent messengers
ahead of him to his brother Esau, toward the land of Seir, the open
country of Edom. [4]He gave them these orders: "Say this to my
master Esau. This is the message of your servant Jacob: 'I've lived
as an immigrant with Laban, where I've stayed till now. [5]I own
cattle, donkeys, flocks, men servants, and women servants. I'm
sending this message to my master now to ask that he[2] be kind.'"

---

1. Or two camps
2. Or you

[6]The messengers returned to Jacob and said, "We went out to your brother Esau, and he's coming to meet you with four hundred men."

[7]Jacob was terrified and felt trapped, so he divided the people with him, and the flocks, cattle, and camels, into two camps. [8]He thought, If Esau meets the first camp and attacks it, at least one camp will be left to escape.

[9]Jacob said, "Lord, God of my father Abraham, God of my father Isaac, who said to me, 'Go back to your country and your relatives, and I'll make sure things go well for you,' [10]I don't deserve how loyal and truthful you've been to your servant. I went away across the Jordan with just my staff, but now I've become two camps. [11]Save me from my brother Esau! I'm afraid he will come and kill me, the mothers, and their children. [12]You were the one who told me, 'I will make sure things go well for you, and I will make your descendants like the sand of the sea, so many you won't be able to count them.'"

[13]Jacob spent that night there. From what he had acquired, he set aside a gift for his brother Esau: [14]two hundred female goats and twenty male goats, two hundred ewes and twenty rams, [15]thirty nursing camels with their young, forty cows and ten bulls, and twenty female donkeys and ten male donkeys. [16]He separated these herds and gave them to his servants. He said to them, "Go ahead of me and put some distance between each of the herds." [17]He ordered the first group, "When my brother Esau meets

you and asks you, 'Who are you with? Where are you going? And whose herds are these in front of you?' [18]say, 'They are your servant Jacob's, a gift sent to my master Esau. And Jacob is actually right behind us.'" [19]He also ordered the second group, the third group, and everybody following the herds, "Say exactly the same thing to Esau when you find him. [20]Say also, 'Your servant Jacob is right behind us.'" Jacob thought, I may be able to pacify Esau with the gift I'm sending ahead. When I meet him, perhaps he will be kind to me. [21]So Jacob sent the gift ahead of him, but he spent that night in the camp.

[22]Jacob got up during the night, took his two wives, his two women servants, and his eleven sons, and crossed the Jabbok River's shallow water. [23]He took them and everything that belonged to him, and he helped them cross the river. [24]But Jacob stayed apart by himself, and a man wrestled with him until dawn broke. [25]When the man saw that he couldn't defeat Jacob, he grabbed Jacob's thigh and tore a muscle in Jacob's thigh as he wrestled with him. [26]The man said, "Let me go because the dawn is breaking."

But Jacob said, "I won't let you go until you bless me."

[27]He said to Jacob, "What's your name?" and he said, "Jacob." [28]Then he said, "Your name won't be Jacob any longer, but Israel,[3] because you struggled with God and with men and won."

[29]Jacob also asked and said, "Tell me your name."

---

3. Or *God struggles* or *one who struggles with God*

But he said, "Why do you ask for my name?" and he blessed Jacob there. [30]Jacob named the place Peniel,[4] "because I've seen God face-to-face, and my life has been saved." [31]The sun rose as Jacob passed Penuel, limping because of his thigh. [32]Therefore, Israelites don't eat the tendon attached to the thigh muscle to this day, because he grabbed Jacob's thigh muscle at the tendon.

INSIGHT AND IDEAS

"Amazing grace! How sweet the sound!"[5]

While most of us have sung those words, many of us have not been soothed by the sweet sound of grace.

I heard a pastor preach, "Our history describes us; it does not define us." But for so many of us, we are imprisoned by our history because we believe that it *does* define us. Our past holds us prisoner from the future that God has in store for us. The deep rooted pain of what we may have done in the past or what has been done to us has turned into shame and often serves as the biggest obstacle that prevents us from moving forward. We may have deemed ourselves unworthy of a promising future; so we resign ourselves to a destiny of shortcomings, putting a limit on how much happiness we deserve. Grace ends up being nothing more than a word in a song. A concept. A theory. A nice sermon.

But grace is so much more than that.

---

4. Or *face of God*
5. From the hymn "Amazing Grace," by John Newton.

As we begin to move forward in our conversations about encountering grace, perhaps the best place is to start is the past; because sometimes we need to go backward to move forward.

As we look back, I hope that you see that God's grace has always been an active presence in your life, that God's grace has always been with you, stirring your heart and drawing you closer to God. Through God's grace, we are more than the sum of our mistakes. No one's history is too dark or too far gone to be redeemed.

JACOB THE DECEIVER

For me, nobody embodies this more than Jacob. Jacob's story is a reminder that we're immersed in God's grace wherever we go, even though we may not be aware of it. But when our hearts are finally open to encounter it, we realize that God's grace has always been with us. And like Jacob, we come to the realization that "the LORD is definitely in this place, but I didn't know it" (Genesis 28:16).

Jacob was not the best of characters; yet, through God's grace, it was Jacob (*not* Esau) whom God chose to be the father of the twelve tribes.

Jacob, which can mean "grasper of heel," got his name because he was born holding on to his brother's heel, as if he were trying to pull Esau back into the womb so that he (Jacob) would be the first born. Grabbing the heel was also a Hebrew way of saying that one was deceiving.

In Jacob's culture, people's names revealed the essence of their soul—who they are and who they will be. You could know a lot about a person (and how he or she should behave) if you knew only his or her name.

But in our culture, you can't tell that much about a person by his or her name. My name is Joseph. That doesn't really tell you anything about me or who I am. Today we tend to make a judgment call on a person based on what he or she does, not on his or her name. For example, if I tell you that I'm a pastor, you begin to know a little bit more about me (and how I should behave). If you were to meet a Jennifer for the first time, you'd know more about her if you learned that she is a doctor than from learning her name.

For the Hebrew culture, everything was in a person's name. People were probably wary around Jacob simply because of what his name meant. And boy, did Jacob live up to his name! (Maybe it was a self-fulfilling prophecy.) For a good portion of his life, Jacob would spend his time and energy tricking and deceiving people, taking what rightfully belonged to them. At one point, after being conned, his brother Esau even screams, "Isn't this why he's called Jacob?" (Genesis 27:36).

ADMITTING WHO WE'VE BEEN

Really, at heart, Jacob was nothing more than a con man—a snake oil salesman. And I have to believe that deep down, Jacob knew this about himself. He tricked his brother out of his birthright. He tricked his father into giving him Esau's inheritance. He conned his father-in-law out of livestock and credited God for his abundance (Genesis 30:37-43).

It is in this context that we find Jacob locked in a grappling match with God (Genesis 32:22-32). And in the midst of the wrestling, God wants to know the name of his opponent. But this goes beyond, "Hey, what's your name?" (After all, God should already know Jacob's name, right?) I believe that God wants Jacob to confess his name— confess the essence of his soul, who he really is; confess his manipulating and conniving ways; confess that he is a shady character; confess that he has wasted his life by devoting his energy and purpose to manipulating others.

And for Jacob to confess—to come clean—was probably more painful than death itself. What does a liar have left when he has no more lies to tell? What is a con man when his ruse is unveiled for all to see?

In the presence of God, Jacob bares all that he is, a deceiver, by admitting that he is Jacob (verse 27). As readers, perhaps we sort of expect punishment to come. I mean, up to this point, what was redeeming about Jacob's character? Jacob has done so many shady things, hurt so many people. He needs to face the consequences of his actions. And now that he has admitted to it all (and to God the judge, no less) justice should be handed out.

FACE TO FACE WITH GRACE

Except, what God says next is not really the justice that we had in mind. When Jacob confesses his name and who he is, God responds by saying, "Your name won't be Jacob any longer, but Israel, because you struggled with God and with men and won" (verse 28).

Wait, what? Jacob went from a deceiver to someone who "struggled with God and with men and *won*" (emphasis mine). That sounds like the furthest thing possible from justice and punishment, the furthest thing from something that Jacob deserves. In fact, it sounds more like a promotion.

And that's the nature of God's grace. God sees you. Not what you have done but *who you are*. Not your past mistakes but your potential. God doesn't see your shortcomings but your capacity to love. God knows you and calls you by name. Your *real name*.

I say, "real name," because we all have different names for ourselves—names that others have given us whether we deserve it or not. (Many of the kids from my youth group called me "Pastor Jerk"—although I'll admit that I proudly earned that name). Or more damning, we have names— ugly names—that we call ourselves because we think that we deserve them.

What are some of the horrible names that you've given yourself? Often, we give those names too much power over us—so much power that they shape, reshape, limit, and even cripple our future.

This was not the first time Jacob was asked who he was. Earlier in Genesis, Jacob was confronted with the same question. At that time, Jacob replied, "I'm Esau your oldest son" (Genesis 27:19). And so Jacob continued his life as a con man.

Perhaps he was tired of running from his past. Perhaps he felt that he would die the next day anyway, since he was confronting the brother he'd wronged. Perhaps he was overwhelmed by the presence of God. For whatever reason, the second time Jacob was asked his name, he confessed, "Jacob."

But when we confess those names to God—when we let grace in—we find that the chains that have been so tightly imprisoning us loosen their grip. We begin to find freedom in God's grace. Once we bring the darkness of those names and expose them to the Light—what "was so powerful while it was in the dark [is] now being exposed and weakened by the light."[6]

And only through confessing was Jacob able to learn the truth—who he was in God's eyes. Everyone else knew him as deceiver, but God knew him as Israel.

PUTTING THE PAST BEHIND US

We tend to put so much weight on our past that it holds us back from moving forward. We try to escape from our past, only to realize that we are running around in circles.

But when we open our heart to God and encounter God's grace, we learn that grace was never an elusive thing that couldn't be obtained, but that it was always there.

---

6. From *Let Hope in: 4 Choices That Will Change Your Life Forever,* by Pete Wilson, (Thomas Nelson, 2013); page 22.

Wherever you were, grace was there. Wherever you are, grace is there. Wherever God calls you, God's grace will go with you. Where can we go to escape the grace of God? "If grace is an ocean, we're all sinking."[7]

May you open your heart and find yourself immersed and in the ocean of God's grace. May you let go of all of the names that have held you captive. In Christ, like Israel, we too have been given a new name—a new identity. For "if anyone is in Christ, that person is part of the new creation. The old things have gone away, and look, new things have arrived!" (2 Corinthians 5:17). God is calling you son, daughter, beloved.

May that realization help shape and guide your journey!

---

7. From the song "How He Loves," by John Mark McMillan.

QUESTIONS

1. Who are God's messengers (Genesis 32:1)? Why are they approaching Jacob?

2. Why does Jacob send his own messengers ahead to meet Esau? Why is Jacob terrified at what they tell him when they return (Genesis 32:3-6)?

3. How is Jacob's prayer to God humble? How is it bold (Genesis 32:9-12)?

4. What does Jacob do to prepare for his meeting with Esau (Genesis 32:13-21)? How does this relate to the prayer Jacob prayed earlier?

5. Why does Jacob want to spend the night away from his family and servants (Genesis 32:22-23)?

6. Who is the mysterious stranger who wrestles with Jacob until dawn (Genesis 32:24)?

7. Why can't the stranger defeat Jacob (Genesis 32:25)? What theological challenges might this passage present?

8. How does the stranger's strength and power compare with Jacob's strength and power (Genesis 32:25-26)?

9. What is the significance of the breaking dawn (Genesis 32:25)? Why does the stranger want to be let go?

10. Why does Jacob want a blessing from the stranger? What does he do to get this blessing (Genesis 32:26-29)? How can we apply this as a principle today?

11. Why does the man ask for Jacob's name but answer with a question when Jacob asks him for *his* name (Genesis 32:27-29)?

12. How does this wrestling match change Jacob? How are we changed when we wrestle with God?

13. Does Jacob get what he deserves in this story? Why, or why not?

2

RETURNING TO GOD
GRACE, REPENTANCE, AND SELF-IMAGE

SCRIPTURE
LUKE 15:11-32

[11]Jesus said, "A certain man had two sons. [12]The younger son said to his father, 'Father, give me my share of the inheritance.' Then the father divided his estate between them. [13]Soon afterward, the younger son gathered everything together and took a trip to a land far away. There, he wasted his wealth through extravagant living.

[14]"When he had used up his resources, a severe food shortage arose in that country and he began to be in need. [15]He hired himself out to one of the citizens of that country, who sent him into his fields to feed pigs. [16]He longed to eat his fill from what the pigs ate, but no one gave him anything. [17]When he came to his senses, he said, 'How many of my father's hired hands have more than enough food, but I'm starving to death! [18]I will get up and go to my father, and say to him, "Father, I have sinned

against heaven and against you. [19]I no longer deserve to be called your son. Take me on as one of your hired hands."' [20]So he got up and went to his father.

"While he was still a long way off, his father saw him and was moved with compassion. His father ran to him, hugged him, and kissed him. [21]Then his son said, 'Father, I have sinned against heaven and against you. I no longer deserve to be called your son.' [22]But the father said to his servants, 'Quickly, bring out the best robe and put it on him! Put a ring on his finger and sandals on his feet! [23]Fetch the fattened calf and slaughter it. We must celebrate with feasting [24]because this son of mine was dead and has come back to life! He was lost and is found!' And they began to celebrate.

[25]"Now his older son was in the field. Coming in from the field, he approached the house and heard music and dancing. [26]He called one of the servants and asked what was going on. [27]The servant replied, 'Your brother has arrived, and your father has slaughtered the fattened calf because he received his son back safe and sound.' [28]Then the older son was furious and didn't want to enter in, but his father came out and begged him. [29]He answered his father, 'Look, I've served you all these years, and I never disobeyed your instruction. Yet you've never given me as much as a young goat so I could celebrate with my friends. [30]But when this son of yours returned, after gobbling up your estate on prostitutes, you slaughtered the fattened calf for him.' [31]Then his father said, 'Son, you are always with me, and everything I have is

yours. [32]But we had to celebrate and be glad because this brother of yours was dead and is alive. He was lost and is found.'"

INSIGHT AND IDEAS

As my wife and I were leaving Staples Center after a Los Angeles Clippers victory (Go, Clippers!), lining the sidewalk outside were people holding picket signs next to a little girl who was speaking through a megaphone. *What in the world could they be protesting,* I wondered. After I read a few signs, I realized that they were picketing *me*. Well, not just me but all of the people leaving the arena.

"You are nothing more than sinners!"

"You're going to hell!"

"The only thing you can do is repent!"

The scene was made slightly eerier by the small girl vocalizing with her sweet, little voice the things written on the signs: "If you don't repent, you will go to hell!"

I had just left the Clippers game. It wasn't like I'd attended an event that was full of evil and soulless people. I would've gone to a Lakers game if I'd wanted that!

MOTIVATED BY FEAR

You see, these folks were trying to motivate me to believe in God out of fear. And unfortunately, fear can be an effective motivator—for a time. The problem is, if it's fear that motivates us into relationship with God, it will probably be fear that is the driving force in the relationship. And a fear-based relationship isn't what God has in mind for us. God's covenant with us isn't built upon fear, but love. "There is no fear in love, but perfect love drives out fear" (1 John 4:18a). It isn't fear of God's wrath and the fire of hell that should lead us to repentance. Paul wrote, "Don't you realize that God's kindness is supposed to lead you to change your heart and life?" (Romans 2:4b).

As we made our way to our car, I began to wonder which came first, grace or repentance?

I assumed that for the picketers, repentance came first then came salvation from the flames of hell—or "grace." But I believe that grace comes before repentance. We don't repent to receive grace; repentance is a response to God's grace.

THE PRODIGAL SON

Nothing really captures that more for me than the powerful story that Jesus told of a wayward, prodigal son. That son had literally declared, "Dad, you're dead to me," by demanding his inheritance here and now. He took his newfound fortune and made his way to a foreign land. We are never told exactly what he did with the money, only that "he wasted his wealth through extravagant living" (Luke 15:13b). He soon found himself broke and desperate to hire himself out for jobs that no one else wanted.

In his desolate and desperate state, he found himself longing for the food he was feeding to pigs. Then a thought struck him: He could ask to have his father hire him as a servant. He surely couldn't go back to him as a son, because he had clearly burned the bridge with his father, family, and village. But coming back as a hired hand might be the perfect solution. The father wouldn't lose face, and the son wouldn't be homeless. On top of that, the son would have food to eat and maybe even earn a small wage. Win-win for everybody.

But he couldn't just show up and say, "Hey, Dad!" He would have to come up with a powerful, sincere apology. I can imagine the son looking at his reflection in a puddle on the pig farm while crafting and practicing his speech.

"Father, I have sinned against heaven and against you. I no longer deserve to be called your son. Take me on as one of your hired hands" (Luke 15:18-19).

Feeling fairly confident about his words, he then makes his way back home.

But "while he was still a long way off, his father saw him and was moved with compassion. His father *ran to him,* hugged him, and kissed him" (Luke 15:20, emphasis mine). What an image!

The father ran toward his son before he even heard the apology. In fact, the father cut off the son mid-apology. Grace came running toward the son before he could even say the words he'd rehearsed. This is a picture of complete acceptance. I've heard it speculated that perhaps the father kissed his son first to prevent the son from kissing the father's hand or feet, which would've been the correct protocol for the son.

UNDERSTANDING REPENTANCE

The son was restored to his rightful place by the unmerited kiss of his father before even uttering a word of repentance. Repentance is important, but grace comes *before* repentance.

You see, that word *repentance* can come with a lot of baggage. Often we tend to associate it with a shopping list of things we have done wrong and need to be forgiven for. And sometimes we repent out of fear, which my friends outside of the Staples Center seemed to be encouraging that night. This can lead many to view God as someone full of wrath who's counting down the days until the punishment for our sins is unleashed. This idea unfortunately leads some to walk away from a god perceived to be so angry and vengeful.

But repentance is much more than what so many of us have made it out to be. One of the Hebrew words for *repent* in the Old Testament, for example, is *shuv,* which means "to turn, return."[1] So when we repent, we return to God; and the image of God within us that has been marred and broken is restored and made whole.

---

1. From "Repentance in the Old Testament," in *The New Interpreter's Dictionary of the Bible,* Volume 4, edited by Katherine Doob Sakenfiel, (Abingdon Press, 2007); page 764.

We don't repent out of fear or only to confess to a laundry list of bad things we've done. We repent to *return* to God. To be made whole by God. To be restored by God. To live the life that God intended for us to live. Grace restores us.

On his trek home, the prodigal son was a fatherless son. He no longer had the freedom that a regular man would have. He saw himself as nothing more than a servant looking for a master to take him in. But when the father saw the young man from a distance, all the father saw was his son coming back home.

GOD SEES US DIFFERENTLY

Grace could not contain itself, so the father ran to his son. Instead of encountering the hostility and anger he'd anticipated, the young man experienced unrestrained love and grace. And with the kiss, he realized that he wasn't going to be a hired servant. He saw that he would always be his father's son, regardless of how much he had marred and distorted that image. The son was made whole through the father's grace.

This theme can be found throughout Scripture. Jacob saw himself as a deceiver, but God saw him as Israel, the father of a chosen nation. Saul saw himself as the destroyer of the Way, but God saw him as the one who would carry the gospel beyond the borders of Jerusalem. Saul was no longer a persecutor of followers of Christ, but instead became one of the biggest champions for God's mission. After being reinstated by Jesus, Peter, the man who could not even admit to a servant girl that he knew Jesus spoke to a crowd, *proclaiming* Jesus. After one meal with Jesus, Zacchaeus went from being a notorious tax collector to being a lavish giver. The Samaritan woman, who had seemingly avoided the people in her village up to that point, dropped everything she had and ran there to proclaim the Messiah after just a single conversation with Jesus.

The story of the prodigal son ends rather abruptly, never resolving the conversation taking place outside of the tent. Nor does Jesus elaborate on what happens to the younger son during the following days.

I'd like to believe that because the father was even more prodigal with his grace than the boy was with money, the younger son lived to be a loving and faithful son, forever changed by what he experienced the day he came back home.

GRACE AND SELF-IMAGE

That journey home started because the young man "came to his senses" (Luke 15:17). He knew that the best option was to come back home—*to return*. But it wasn't his father's kindness that led him to return; it was his desperation. His image of himself was so broken and distorted that in his own mind, he was nothing more than a hired servant—that was all that he was good for, all that he was worth. And because his self-image was distorted, the image of his father was distorted as well. He could only see a man who would be angry with him.

But grace altered the broken image that the young man had of himself. Grace restored his sonship. Grace brought new life out of death. And I believe that because of that, the young son began to live the life that he had been intended to live. When God's grace and kindness lead us to repentance, we are forever changed because our view of ourselves has changed. It's then that we know who we really are: sons and daughters of God. The power of grace leads us to abandon the road of self-living and forgo the idea of controlling our own fate and lives.

Grace gives us new life. Grace shows us that we are truly created in the image of God. And what we now see can never be unseen again.

So like Paul, Israel, Zacchaeus, the Samaritan woman, the adulteress, and many more, we move forward, confronted by the mirror that grace holds up for us. However, the reflections don't show the sum of our mistakes; but the amazing truth that "we are God's heirs and fellow heirs with Christ" (Romans 8:17b).

However lost we may feel, we are always found in grace.

QUESTIONS

1. Why did the father give the younger son his share of the inheritance while the father was still alive (Luke 15:12)?

2. What is the significance of the "land far away" (Luke 15:13)?

3. What can we conclude from the younger son's job situation in the distant country (Luke 15:15)?

4. What made the younger son "[come] to his senses" (Luke 15:17)? Do you believe that he was truly sorry at this point for what he'd done? Why, or why not?

5. What did the son mean by, "I have sinned against heaven and against you" (Luke 15:18)?

6. What was different about the son's actual speech from the way he'd rehearsed it (Luke 15:18-19, 21)?

7. Why was the older son so angry (Luke 15:28)? Why don't we find out how the older son responded to the father's plea to join the celebration?

8. Who do the various characters in this story represent? What roles have you played from this story in the past?

9. What are the problems that come with using fear as a motivator for faith?

10. Do you agree with the author's assertion that grace comes before repentance? Why, or why not?

11. What is the connection between our self-image and receiving God's grace?

12. What can Christians learn from this passage about how to treat other believers?

3

MISUNDERSTANDING GRACE
JUSTIFICATION IS ONLY THE BEGINNING

SCRIPTURE
ROMANS 6:1-23

¹So what are we going to say? Should we continue sinning so grace will multiply? ²Absolutely not! All of us died to sin. How can we still live in it? ³Or don't you know that all who were baptized into Christ Jesus were baptized into his death? ⁴Therefore, we were buried together with him through baptism into his death, so that just as Christ was raised from the dead through the glory of the Father, we too can walk in newness of life. ⁵If we were united together in a death like his, we will also be united together in a resurrection like his. ⁶This is what we know: the person that we used to be was crucified with him in order to get rid of the corpse that had been controlled by sin. That way we wouldn't be slaves to

sin anymore, [7]because a person who has died has been freed from sin's power. [8]But if we died with Christ, we have faith that we will also live with him. [9]We know that Christ has been raised from the dead and he will never die again. Death no longer has power over him. [10]He died to sin once and for all with his death, but he lives for God with his life. [11]In the same way, you also should consider yourselves dead to sin but alive for God in Christ Jesus.

[12]So then, don't let sin rule your body, so that you do what it wants. [13]Don't offer parts of your body to sin, to be used as weapons to do wrong. Instead, present yourselves to God as people who have been brought back to life from the dead, and offer all the parts of your body to God to be used as weapons to do right. [14]Sin will have no power over you, because you aren't under Law but under grace.

[15]So what? Should we sin because we aren't under Law but under grace? Absolutely not! [16]Don't you know that if you offer yourselves to someone as obedient slaves, that you are slaves of the one whom you obey? That's true whether you serve as slaves of sin, which leads to death, or as slaves of the kind of obedience that leads to righteousness. [17]But thank God that although you used to be slaves of sin, you gave wholehearted obedience to the teaching that was handed down to you, which provides a pattern. [18]Now that you have been set free from sin, you have become slaves of righteousness. [19](I'm speaking with ordinary metaphors because of your limitations.) Once, you offered the parts of your body to be used as slaves to impurity and to lawless behavior that

leads to still more lawless behavior. Now, you should present the parts of your body as slaves to righteousness, which makes your lives holy. [20]When you were slaves of sin, you were free from the control of righteousness. [21]What consequences did you get from doing things that you are now ashamed of? The outcome of those things is death. [22]But now that you have been set free from sin and become slaves to God, you have the consequence of a holy life, and the outcome is eternal life. [23]The wages that sin pays are death, but God's gift is eternal life in Christ Jesus our Lord.

INSIGHT AND IDEAS

Imagine that you're sitting at your favorite coffee shop. You're trying to read but your ears perk up because the couple sitting next to you is being a bit loud. You try not to listen; but because of their volume, it's almost like they're inviting you into their conversation.

The ring on the woman's finger gives you a clue that the couple might be engaged, but somehow they seem to be caught up in the dreaded DTR talk (Define-the-Relationship, for the uninitiated). The conversation you're hearing is far more engaging than the words in front of you, so you pretend to read. But your ears are latching on to every spoken word.

"So," begins the woman after a few moments of silence. "Now that we're engaged and about to get married, what would you consider to be cheating?"

"What?" her fiancé almost shouts.

"Like, if I were to give a lingering hug to another guy, would that be cheating? Or what if I'm hanging out with my girls, and I've had one too many drinks and I kiss another guy? Or how about a peck on the cheek? Or a quick smooch to the guy who bought me a drink? Would you be upset? Would that be cheating? I guess sleeping with someone else would probably count as cheating, but would that be such a big deal?"

"*What?* Of course!" he replies, seething.

"Wait, don't get mad. I'm just trying to figure everything out. What if it was someone really hot? What if I hooked up with Ryan Gosling? Or someone that *you* like—like Wolverine, Batman, or Thor? Wouldn't you be more proud of me than upset? I mean, sure, you might be hurt at first; but think about all the chances you'll get to prove your unconditional love by forgiving me over and over."

After hearing a few minutes of this ludicrous conversation, it would be fair to say that this woman has reservations about a long-term commitment and doesn't know much about staying in love. You might even wonder whether she has ever even experienced real love. When the woman gets up to go to the restroom, you might advise the young man to run as far and fast as he can from her. Who knows? You could be on the TV show *What Would You Do?* You wouldn't want to be that person who overheard everything and did nothing to help this guy.

WHAT CAN I GET AWAY WITH?

This illustration reminds me of the game I played with God all the time when I was young: "How much can I get away with and still be a Christian?" OK, fine, I still play it. But the question has evolved slightly. It's now, "How much can I get away with and still be a *good* Christian?" (That *good* makes a huge difference.) The "How much can I get away with?" question is a very dear cousin to "It's OK, God's going to forgive me anyhow."

Maybe because grace is so amazing, we don't know how to comprehend it or what to do with it. We may end up treating it like the collector's Superman action figure (not doll!) that I have unopened and untouched in its package on a shelf in my church office—its only purpose being to be looked at and to increase in value as its packaging collects dust. For the most part, I forget that Superman is standing there (next to the Buddy Jesus figure). Once in a while, I'll take his box off the shelf, dust it off, and make sure that it is still unopened. And every so often, I'll search the Internet to see how much he's worth. If I'm ever in desperate need for a tank of gas or extra cash, I could always sell him.

So, like the action figure, we sort of let grace sit there, collecting dust; and we pull it out when we desperately need it, like a get-out-of-jail-free card. Or we end up using grace as a license to sin. I mean, Christ died for my sins, right? Since my sins are already forgiven, what is stopping me? Paul asks the same question, "Should we continue sinning so grace will multiply?" (Romans 6:1b). "Absolutely

43

not!" answers Paul in the next verse. For someone who abuses grace in this way, we have to ask whether he or she has ever truly encountered grace. Pastor Judah Smith writes, "People who flaunt their sin in the name of grace don't know what grace is."[1]

BEGINNING OF A JOURNEY

Maybe one of the reasons we so easily misuse grace is because we put too much emphasis on being saved, as if that's the ultimate goal of our faith. During my college days, I got involved in a ministry when I accidentally showed up to one of their gatherings. My keen sense of direction had led me to the wrong place. Unaware of where I was, I signed in and gave those folks my phone number. When someone stood in the front and said, "Let us pray," I realized that I was in the wrong place. I was not even supposed to be at a Christian gathering that day. I couldn't sneak out, and on top of that, they had my information now. It took months of hard work using my crafty ninja skills of avoiding people and screening calls to get them to leave me alone.

These guys were all about saving souls. That was their mission. That was their goal. When they were able to get someone to recite the Sinner's Prayer and accept Jesus Christ as their Lord and Savior, there wasn't much of a follow-up. The new converts were sent right back out to save more souls. But they didn't seem very "Christian" in

---

1. From *Jesus Is _____*, by Judah Smith, (Thomas Nelson, 2013); Page 50.

their words and actions. When I finally got the courage to answer one of their calls to end whatever relationship we had, they basically wished me luck when I went to hell. They acted like bullies, saying and doing whatever they pleased, resting on their laurels of salvation. I guess they figured that they could do no wrong because they were assured of their salvation; they had already RSVP'd their seat at heaven's dining table.

This group had achieved their goal as Christians: *Why try hard to be a better person when God has already accepted me and saved me? My work is done. I am saved. I can now just live using this newfound freedom of salvation as a license to say or do anything I want. My salvation is secured, so I can just hang out until Jesus comes back and takes me home.* They saw themselves as invincible to sin because they were under grace.

My biggest disagreement with them was that I believed, and still strongly believe, that salvation—being saved—is not the goal or end of our journey. It is the beginning of a new, fantastic journey.

JUSTIFYING GRACE

Being "converted" or being "saved" is what John Wesley would call *justifying grace*. We are aware of God's mercy and grace and are led to repentance (to return to God). Grace, then, resurrects us to the life that God always intended for us to live. "Therefore, we were buried together with him through baptism into his death, so that just as

Christ was raised from the dead through the glory of the Father, we too can *walk in newness of life*" (Romans 6:4, emphasis mine). There is a newness of life to explore, to experience, to live. Our salvation doesn't end with reciting a prayer and accepting Jesus Christ as our Lord and Savior. Salvation marks the beginning of a new journey together, God and us.

But being found alive in grace doesn't give us the freedom to live our lives however we see fit. Paul reminds us, "You were called to freedom, brothers and sisters; only don't let this freedom be an opportunity to indulge your selfish impulses, but serve each other through love" (Galatians 5:13). As Wesley would say, we are now working toward perfection, being sustained by God's grace to live a life that is purpose-filled and grace-filled affecting our world through the things that God is doing through us—partnering with God in unleashing God's love throughout our communities.

IN LOVE WITH GOD

Maybe another reason why we abuse/misuse grace is that we simply aren't in love with God. Back to the imaginary couple illustration: If the woman were truly in love, she wouldn't try to figure out ways to exploit that love. She wouldn't be debating, bartering, or trying to see what she could get away with. That isn't love.

Love is sacrificial by nature and drives us to make sacrifices. And who has shown more sacrificial love than God through Jesus Christ?

When we think, "Can I get away with this?" or "God's going to forgive me anyway," we aren't in love with God. In fact, we don't even know God. Nor do we understand grace. We may grasp an idea or concept. But we haven't experienced Christ, nor have we encountered grace. Instead, we've embraced the idea that God is more interested in what we do than in the condition of our hearts.

When our hearts aren't in something, we try to compensate with our actions and our performance. But God doesn't want a performance or a show. God wants our heart. God wants *us*. Trying to be good is secondary. *Love* is what motivates us to be holy.

When we encounter grace, we're resurrected from our deadness; our relationship and life with God are restored to their original intent. Now, we move forward, fully aware of our partnership with God, ready to live out the vision and purpose God has for us. God's grace leads us on our journey toward perfection, because God loves us too much to let us stay the same.

QUESTIONS

1. What does it mean to die to sin (Romans 6:2)? Is this a one time event or a process? Explain your answer.

2. What is the connection between baptism and sin (Romans 6:3-4)?

3. How are human beings slaves to sin? When do we stop being slaves to sin (Romans 6:7)?

4. How do we consider ourselves dead to sin (Romans 6:11)? What does this look like, practically speaking?

5. What does it mean to let sin rule over us? How do we stop this from happening (Romans 6:12)?

6. What is the connection between the Law, grace, and sin's power over us (Romans 6:14)?

7. Compare and contrast being a slave to sin to being a slave to righteousness. Why does Paul use the slavery metaphor for both sin and righteousness? Is it possible to be a slave to neither (Romans 6:18)?

8. What are the limitations that Paul might be referring to in Romans 6:19?

9. What does it mean to live a holy life? How is this connected to eternal life (Romans 6:22)?

10. Paul speaks of both wages and a gift in Romans 6:23. What point might he have been trying to make by using these specific terms?

11. Why is it important to avoid a faith that searches for loopholes and asks, "What can I get away with?" What would the opposite extreme of this error be?

12. What do you mean when you use the term *salvation*? How might this term be confusing or ambiguous?

13. How can Christians make sure that they're "in love with God"? What are some steps that can be taken to maintain and grow in this relationship?

14. How do Christians misuse or abuse grace today?

4

FROM THE INSIDE OUT
GOD'S GRACE AND THE HUMAN HEART

SCRIPTURE
EPHESIANS 2:1-16

[1]At one time you were like a dead person because of the things you did wrong and your offenses against God. [2]You used to live like people of this world. You followed the rule of a destructive spiritual power. This is the spirit of disobedience to God's will that is now at work in persons whose lives are characterized by disobedience. [3]At one time you were like those persons. All of you used to do whatever felt good and whatever you thought you wanted so that you were children headed for punishment just like everyone else.

[4-5]However, God is rich in mercy. He brought us to life with Christ while we were dead as a result of those things that we did wrong. He did this because of the great love that he has for us. You are saved by God's grace! [6]And God raised us up and seated

us in the heavens with Christ Jesus. [7]God did this to show future generations the greatness of his grace by the goodness that God has shown us in Christ Jesus.

[8]You are saved by God's grace because of your faith.[1] This salvation is God's gift. It's not something you possessed. [9]It's not something you did that you can be proud of. [10]Instead, we are God's accomplishment, created in Christ Jesus to do good things. God planned for these good things to be the way that we live our lives.

[11]So remember that once you were Gentiles by physical descent, who were called "uncircumcised" by Jews who are physically circumcised. [12]At that time you were without Christ. You were aliens rather than citizens of Israel, and strangers to the covenants of God's promise. In this world you had no hope and no God. [13]But now, thanks to Christ Jesus, you who once were so far away have been brought near by the blood of Christ.

[14]Christ is our peace. He made both Jews and Gentiles into one group. With his body, he broke down the barrier of hatred that divided us. [15]He canceled the detailed rules of the Law so that he could create one new person out of the two groups, making peace. [16]He reconciled them both as one body to God by the cross, which ended the hostility to God.

---

1. Or *through his faithfulness*

INSIGHT AND IDEAS

Grace can be a troubling subject for many of us. We talk about it more than we practice it, and we receive it more than we give it. Because grace is so powerful and so amazing, it's hard to think that someone we deem undeserving receives it for free. *There's no such thing as "free" in this world,* we remind ourselves. (Never mind that we did nothing to deserve it, either.) But we also understand that although grace is given freely, it came at a great cost. It cost Jesus his life.

So we sometimes start imposing conditions to this free gift. But if we are not careful, we may find ourselves the way Jesus found the Pharisees when he said, "Don't do what they do. For they tie together heavy packs that are impossible to carry. They put them on the shoulders of others, but are unwilling to lift a finger to move them" (Matthew 23:3b-4).

'US' AND 'THEM'

For a long period of my life, I didn't understand what people meant when they said, "I believe in Jesus, but I'm not religious." Jesus and religion were so intertwined in my belief, I couldn't fathom one without the other.

But as I grow in my faith, I see how religion often gets in the way of Jesus. Please don't misunderstand. I'm not saying that religion is bad and that we should do away with *all* religious things. Religion is good and important. It's just that religion has a tendency to act as a hurdle over the mission and purpose of Jesus. Religion draws a subtle line in the sand that puts people into two categories: "us" and "them." We are far more lenient to those who are with us, overlooking their shortcomings and overselling their good qualities.

Likewise, we are more critical and harsher toward "them," overlooking their good qualities and intensely focusing on their shortcomings. "We" have specks of dust in our eye; "they" have the plank in theirs!

When one of "them" sees the light and becomes one of "us," instead of celebrating, we give them more rules to follow—a bigger burden to shoulder—and we tell them that it is a cross they have to bear for the sake of Jesus. We appoint ourselves the Sheriff of Grace, who decides how one can receive God's grace and when one can receive it.

So instead of being a sanctuary for those who might not feel good about themselves, we (the church) end up putting the world's biggest magnifying glass on their lowest and/or worst moments for all to see and judge—all in the name of God's grace.

RULES VERSUS GRACE

For me, religion has become much more synonymous with rules than with grace. Religion focuses a lot of energy and time on one's outer layer, one's behavior. Religion tells us what we cannot do and what we should do, which is important and necessary. But this is why many people walk away from religion, feeling empty, bitter, guilty, and/or full of shame, unable to keep up with all of the rules.

Jesus came to do something drastically different. While religion tries to change someone *from the outside in,* Jesus came to change us *from the inside out.* He is more focused on restoring our hearts than curbing our behavior. When we drive our focus and energy on rules and external behaviors, we are implying that our actions—what we do or what we say—are far more important than who we are as human beings.

When I was a teenager, I once got into trouble (a rare occurrence). I was expecting a long lecture from my father about how I messed up, how I was not being a good son—yada, yada, yada—and what my punishment would be. Instead, he looked at me and said, "You're a Yoo. And Yoos don't behave like this." That hit home for me more than any punishment I could have received. My dad was telling me who I was and that I was created for something more, something better.

WHERE GRACE STARTS

I believe that is where the grace of Jesus starts—with who we are—and builds from there: You are a child of God; you are created for something more, something better. Religion, on the other hand, starts with who we are not: You are not good and need to be saved, so start doing these things in the hope that you will be good enough one day.

Throughout the Gospels, the religious thing to do was to separate oneself from notorious sinners, such as the tax collectors, lepers, prostitutes, and Samaritans. But Jesus *ate with them*—so many times that "the Pharisees and legal experts were grumbling, saying, 'This man welcomes sinners and eats with them'" (Luke 15:2). The religious thing to do was to stone the adulteress. But Jesus said that he did not condemn her, and he urged her to not sin anymore.

I am reminded through Jesus that grace often trumps rules, ideologies, and theologies.

Like religion, Jesus also draws a subtle line in the sand. Instead of dividing people into "us" versus "them," he grouped people into "sinners who admit and sinners who deny."[2] Jesus preferred to spend time with "sinners who admit" because there wasn't a false pretense of righteousness within them. They knew they needed God. The righteous, however, needed to be acknowledged as such from other people. As Jesus said, "I assure you, that's the only reward they'll get."

EMPTY GOOD DEEDS

For the righteous of Jesus' day and the religious of today, our insistent adherence to the rules leads us to be full of empty good deeds.

"'God, I thank you that I'm not like everyone else—crooks, evildoers, adulterers—or even like this tax collector. I fast twice a week. I give a tenth of everything I receive'" (Luke 18:11-12).

---

2. From *What's So Amazing About Grace?* by Philip Yancey, (Zondervan, 1997), ePub edition.

I go to church every Sunday.

I volunteer even when I don't want to.

I don't curse.

I don't drink.

I don't watch R-rated movies.

I don't listen to secular music.

I don't do or sell drugs.

I am a good person because of the things I do and do not do.

C.S. Lewis wrote, "St. Augustine says 'God gives where he finds empty hands.' A man whose hands are full of parcels can't receive a gift."[3] Are our hearts and hands too full of empty good deeds that we have no room to receive grace?

Empty good deeds can make us feel superior to our neighbors. They also tend to make everything about *us,* to the point where we start thinking that our salvation is dependent on what we do and not on God's actions. So we place our trust not in God, but in the rules and our ability to keep them.

However, Paul refutes this notion in his Epistles.

> You are saved by God's grace because of your faith. This
> salvation is God's gift. It's not something you possessed. It's
> not something you did that you can be proud of. Instead, we

---

3. From *The Collected Letters of C.S. Lewis, Volume 3: Narnia, Cambridge, and Joy,* by C.S. Lewis, edited by Walter Hooper, (Zondervan, 2007); eBook edition; pages 930–931.

are God's accomplishment, created in Christ Jesus to do good things. God planned for these good things to be the way that we live our lives. (Ephesians 2:8-10)

However, we know that a person isn't made righteous by the works of the Law but rather through the faithfulness of Jesus Christ. We ourselves believed in Christ Jesus. . . . I don't ignore the grace of God, because if we become righteous through the Law, then Christ died for no purpose. (Galatians 2:16a, 21)

Adherence to rules is about *me* and what I have accomplished. Grace is about God's action through Jesus. Grace shows us that God loves us not because of anything we have done or who we are, but because God is God.

"God shows his love for us, because while we were still sinners Christ died for us" (Romans 5:8).

It is never about us. It is always about God and what God did, does, and will continue to do through God's people.

REAL CHANGE

Focusing on changing someone from the outside in—behavior modification—can go only so far. Real change comes from within, from the heart. Grace can melt the hardest of hearts, and love can change even the most stubborn of hearts.

God showed love for us through Jesus Christ. Our response should go beyond keeping rules or signing a contract. Besides, we don't have a contract anyway; we have a covenant. And this covenant is based upon and driven by love.

St. Augustine wrote, "Love [God], and do what you will."[4]
He knew that if we earnestly love God, we will be inclined
to honor God. Rules would be secondary to love. Love
is the true motivator. That is why Jesus told us that the
greatest commandment is "Love the Lord your God with
all your heart, with all your being, and with all your mind"
(Matthew 22:37; Deuteronomy 6:5[5]).

Grace is God's gift to us. May our hands be empty to receive
it. May our hearts be filled, not with empty good deeds,
but with God's love and grace. May we allow God's grace
to restore us and shape us into the person we were created
to be. May we be extensions of God's grace and love to
our communities, showing others the same grace that we
have been shown. My prayer is that the melody of grace will
always be the song that our hearts sing. "Amazing grace!
How sweet the sound!"[6]

---

4. From "Homily 7, Section 8," in *Homilies on the First Epistle of John,* by Saint Augustine,
translated by H. Browne, from *Nicene and Post-Nicene Fathers,* First Series, Volume 7. Edited by
Philip Schaff, (Christian Literature Publishing Co., 1888). Revised and edited for New Advent by
Kevin Knight. *http://www.newadvent.org/fathers/1702.htm.* Accessed 7 April 2014.
5. Deuteronomy 6:5 uses the word *strength* instead of *mind.*
6. From the hymn "Amazing Grace," by John Newton.

QUESTIONS

1. What are "offenses against God"? When were we "like dead people" (Ephesians 2:1)?

2. What is the "spirit of disobedience" (Ephesians 2:2)? What implications might this verse have for personal responsibility?

3. What is the punishment Ephesians 2:3 refers to? Is it still in effect? Whom is this punishment for?

4. What is God's mercy? How do we receive it (Ephesians 2:4-5)?

5. In what ways are we "seated . . . in the heavens with Christ Jesus"? What exactly does this mean (Ephesians 2:6)?

6. Why is it important for future generations to know about the greatness of God's grace (Ephesians 2:7)? What role do we play in that?

7. How does God's grace save us? What does it save us from (Ephesians 2:8)?

8. Why shouldn't we be proud of our salvation (Ephesians 2:9)?

9. How does Jesus make people into one group today (Ephesians 2:14)? How are we resisting that?

10. Ephesians 2:15 tells us that God "canceled the detailed rules of the Law." Practically, what does this mean for believers today?

11. Why is grace often easier to receive than it is to give? Are there situations where the reverse is true? Explain.

12. If obeying rules doesn't save us, what role, if any, do rules have in the life of a believer?

13. Is it possible to abuse God's grace or take it for granted? If so, how?

Check out Joseph Yoo's other title in the Converge series!

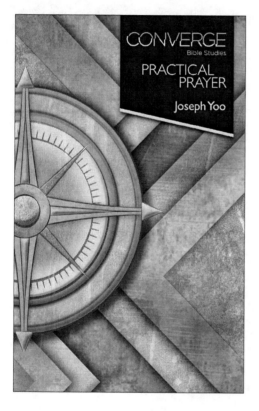

Practical Prayer
Joseph Yoo
9781426778254, Print
9781426778291, eBook

 Abingdon Press™

BKM146600011 PACP01479639-01

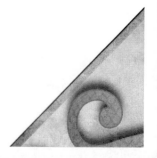

CPSIA information can be obtained at www.ICGtesting.com
Printed in the USA
LVOW05s0828110414

381199LV00003B/4/P

CONVERGE

Bible Studies

CONVERGE is where life and faith come together.

Grace can be a troubling subject for many of us. We talk about it more than we practice it, and we receive it more than we give it. Because grace is so powerful and so amazing, it's hard to think that someone we deem undeserving receives it for free. But real grace is both liberating and contagious. Once we truly experience it, we become different people. And the further we journey in our faith, the more we realize the role God's grace has played in our lives—even before we came to faith in Christ. *Encountering Grace* is a study about learning to receive God's grace as well as offer that grace to others.

Converge Bible Studies is a series of topical Bible studies. Each title in the series consists of four studies on a common topic or theme. *Converge* can be used by small groups, classes, or individuals. Primary Scripture passages from the Common English Bible are included for ease of study, as are questions designed to encourage both personal reflection and group conversation. The topics and Scriptures in *Converge* come together to transform readers' relationships with others, themselves, and God.

Joseph Yoo has a passion for affecting the world by making the message and love of Christ relevant to his community and beyond. Joseph and his wife, Rahel, live in Santa Barbara, California, where he serves as pastor of St. Mark United Methodist Church. Joseph really likes music, movies, and the Washington Redskins.

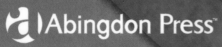

Abingdon Press™

www.abingdonpress.com

Cover Design: Matt Orozco

Religion/Bible Studies/Bible Study Guide $9.99

ISBN-13: 978-1-4267-9553-

50999

9 781426 795534